IMAGES
of America

EAST TEXAS IN
WORLD WAR II

Even in Italy, Texans in the 36th Division, the "Texas Army," were always aware of how far away they were from the Lone Star state. (Courtesy of the Texas Military Forces Museum at Camp Mabry, Austin.)

ON THE COVER: With generally clear skies and favorable weather, Texas was an obvious training site for airmen. Over 200,000 fliers, more than in any other state, trained at 40 air bases in Texas. Essential personnel at every base were airplane mechanics, such as this crew on duty at Terrell in Northeast Texas. (Courtesy of the No.1 British Flying Training Field Museum, Terrell, Texas.)

IMAGES
of America

EAST TEXAS IN
WORLD WAR II

Bill O'Neal

ARCADIA
PUBLISHING

Published by Arcadia Publishing
Charleston, South Carolina

Printed in the United States of America

Library of Congress Control Number: 2010926107

For all general information, please contact Arcadia Publishing:
Telephone 843-853-2070
Fax 843-853-0044
E-mail sales@arcadiapublishing.com
For customer service and orders:
Toll-Free 1-888-313-2665

Visit us on the Internet at www.arcadiapublishing.com

For my twin grandchildren: Reagan O'Neal and Nolan Drew Gormley

CONTENTS

ACKNOWLEDGMENTS

When I launched this pictorial study of East Texas in World War II, I spent several weeks traveling through the eastern third of Texas. I visited museums, libraries, the campus of Texas A&M University, memorials in towns large and small, and the sites of training bases, military hospitals, and POW camps. Everywhere I received enthusiastic assistance. During nearly four decades of teaching history at Panola College in Carthage, I received from my students hundreds of interviews with World War II veterans or with those who manned the home front in East Texas. Those interviews provided a wealth of information, and I am grateful to my former students for providing this accumulation of experiences to me from their fathers, grandfathers, other relatives, and family friends.

I deeply appreciate the help I received from the following: Ross Mohr, corps captain at Texas A&M; Dennis Johnson at Camp Mabry in Austin; Susan Lanning, director of the Audie Murphy/ American Cotton Museum in Greenville; Henry Madgwick, Freida Freeman, and Mike Grout of the No. 1 British Flying Training Museum in Terrell; David Stroud, history faculty of Kilgore College; John and Betty Oglesbee of San Augustine; Dusty Henderson of Van Alstyne; Dr. Shellie O'Neal of Navarro College in Corsicana; Kent Brunette, director of the Hearne Chamber of Commerce; Cathy Lazarus, director of the Camp Hearne Museum; Dr. Beverly Rowe of Texarkana College; Sam Kidd and Mary Jane McNamara of the Smith County Historical Society, Tyler; Emily Hobson, research librarian of the Marshall Public Library; author Bob Bowman of Lufkin; Liz Gant, director of the Seagoville Public Library; Sherri Baker, research librarian at Panola College in Carthage; Albert Richards of Henderson; Tanya Wilkes, graphics manager of Complete Printing in Carthage; Joe White, director of the East Texas Oil Museum in Kilgore; Joe Bell of Longview; and staff members of the Gregg County Museum in Longview.

For entrusting me with photographs of their fathers and grandfathers, as well as with other artifacts and family information, I am grateful to the following: Shirly Bruton Ford of San Jose, California; and in Texas, Judy O'Neal Smith of Lampasas, Dr. Berri O'Neal Gormley of Dallas, Faye Gipson Frasier of Corpus Christi, and Dr. Donna Otterman Porter, Drew Darnell, and Cliff Todd, all of Carthage.

I am indebted to Luke Cunningham of Arcadia Publishing for successfully promoting the concept of this book with the publishers, and I am grateful to Hannah Carney for her editorial expertise on behalf of this project.

My wife, Karon, was of indispensable help, as always. She was a reliable sounding board, encourager, and photographic assistant, and she converted my manuscript to acceptable forms for the publisher. I could not have met the book deadline without her efforts.

INTRODUCTION

Texas made extraordinary contributions to the American war effort during World War II. Manpower, combat exploits, upper-level military leadership, wartime industries, oil production—all were out of proportion to the relative population size and contributions of Texas compared to the other 47 states.

Almost 830,000 Texans, including 12,000 women, donned uniforms, representing more than 7 percent of the overall total, even though the Texas population (6.4 million in 1940) comprised only 5 percent of the U. S. population. Indeed, by the percentage of the Texas population, more Texans served in World War II than any other state. More than 23,000 Texans died for their country—7 percent of the overall American total.

For over a century, Texas men had been expected to defend their homes from Mexican soldiers, border raiders, Comanche and Kiowa war parties, rustlers, and feudists. During the Civil War, out of the 92,000 Texas men between the ages of 18 and 45, more than 60,000 joined Confederate forces. There was a large Texan turnout during the war with Spain and World War I, and Texans continued their ingrained habit of military service during World War II.

America's most decorated soldier, Lt. Audie Murphy, and the most decorated sailor, submarine commander Sam Dealey, were both Texans, and so was Sgt. Jim Logan, regarded by many as America's second-most decorated soldier. More than 30 other Texans also won the Congressional Medal of Honor.

Seven men who earned the Medal of Honor were Texas Aggies. Texas A&M, an all-male military college, placed over 20,000 men in the armed forces, more than any other college or university, including the U.S. Military Academy at West Point. Over 14,000 Aggies were commissioned officers, including 29 generals. Texas Aggies served during the doomed defense of Corregidor. Five Aggies were among 80 fliers during the Doolittle Raid on Tokyo. Lt. Col. Earl Rudder led the Ranger assault on Pointe du Hoc during the D-Day invasion of Normandy. Aggies served on every battlefront of the war, and more than 900 died.

The 36th Division was a Texas National Guard unit that was federalized in both world wars. Known as the "Texas Division" and the "Texas Army," the 36th saw heavy combat in Europe, suffering more than 19,000 killed, wounded, and captured. The 90th Division, also activated in both world wars, was originally manned by men from Texas and Oklahoma. Called "Texas' Own," "Tough 'Ombres," and the "Alamo Division," this motorized division fought in Europe and suffered almost as many casualties as the 36th Division.

On the senior leadership level, more than 150 generals and 12 admirals were Texans. Gen. Dwight David Eisenhower, supreme commander of Allied Forces in Europe, was born in Denison in Northeast Texas. Adm. Chester Nimitz, commander in chief of U.S. Naval Forces in the Pacific (CINCPAC), was born and raised in Fredericksburg. Another Texan, Gen. Ira Eaker, led the famous Eighth Air Force in Europe and was instrumental in developing the strategy of daylight precision bombing. Gen. Claire Chennault, born in Commerce in Northeast Texas, organized and commanded the colorful "Flying Tigers" in China.

Col. Oveta Culp Hobby of Houston, wife of former governor William P. Hobby and an accomplished woman in her own right, was appointed to organize and lead the Women's Army Auxiliary Corps (WAACs, later the Women's Army Corps—WACs). More than 12,000 Texas women served in the WACs, WAVES (Women Appointed for Voluntary Emergency Services), WASPs (Women's Airforce Service Pilots), WAFS (Women's Auxiliary Ferry Squadron), U.S. Women Marines, SPARs (from *semper paratus*, "always prepared," the motto of the U.S. Coast Guard), and in the Nursing Corps of the U.S. Army and of the U.S. Navy. The nation's only all-female training base, Avenger Field in Sweetwater, was home to the WASPs.

Texas had over 80 military bases. There were 19 army bases, 65 airfields, and 4 naval stations. Texas was America's largest training field. Beginning in 1940, twenty combat divisions were trained in Texas. With its clear skies and generally favorable weather, all military airmen were trained in Texas until 1938, and during the war, 200,000 pilots, navigators, bombardiers, and gunners received their training at the many airfields, large and small, in the Lone Star state. Almost 1.5 million military personnel were trained in Texas. Over 50,000 prisoners of war were housed in compounds on large bases and in POW camps around the state.

A key element to American victory in World War II was the prodigious production of planes, ships, tanks, and the other tools of war. The industrial buildup began before American entry into the war, and by 1943, the great machine was in full stride. Indeed, by 1944, America was producing double the combined totals of the enemy countries. Production totals were astounding: 296,400 airplanes; 86,330 tanks; 2,681,000 machine guns; 6,500 naval vessels; 5,400 cargo ships and troop transports; 64,500 landing craft; and 25,065,834,000 rounds of .30-caliber ammunition.

Texas played a major role in these miracles of production, with long-term results for the future. The Lone Star Army Ammunition Plant and Red River Army Depot in Texarkana and another Lone Star Army Ammunition Plant in Harrison County sent a flood of munitions from Northeast Texas. Airplane plants in Dallas, Garland, Fort Worth, and other North Texas locations assembled AT-6s, P-51s, and B-24s—trainers, fighters, and bombers. Shipyards in Houston, Galveston, Port Arthur, Orange, and Corpus Christi manufactured destroyer escorts, Liberty ships, and seagoing vessels. The Ford plant in Dallas produced 100,000 jeeps and army trucks.

By the start of the war, Texas produced 40 percent of U.S. oil and 25 percent of world oil, while 40 percent of American refineries were located in the Lone Star state. Along the coast, the world's greatest petrochemical industry developed.

With the young men of Texas entering the military by the hundreds of thousands, manufacturing jobs went to women, older men, black Texans, Hispanics, and rural Texans. Almost 500,000 Texans moved from the country to urban areas to take up jobs that offered good pay, including production bonuses, overtime, and double overtime.

At least 450,000 out-of-state workers gravitated to war industry jobs in Texas. Many of them stayed in Texas after the war, while a large number of veterans who had been stationed in the Lone Star state relocated to this region of mild winters and great opportunity. World War II was a major step in the transformation of a rural and agricultural Texas to an industrial and urban giant.

Within just 128 pages, it is impossible to detail each of the thousands of men and women of East Texas who donned uniforms, to depict the countless heroic exploits of East Texans, or to describe the scores of military bases and defense plants and POW camps in the eastern third of Texas. The following pages will portray highlights of the war years, a cross-section of a valiant and triumphant era for East Texans.

One

TEXAS ENTERS THE WAR

The Second World War erupted in September 1939 in Europe. Although more than two years would pass before the United States entered the war, Pres. Franklin D. Roosevelt pushed an American military buildup, calling for a $1-billion defense appropriation in May 1940. National Guard units were activated, and in September 1940, Congress adopted the first peacetime draft in American history. Above, a Texas National Guard rifle company is on the firing range at Camp Bowie in March 1941. (Courtesy of Camp Mabry.)

With a long background of frontier violence and warfare, Texans were alarmed by the aggressions of Hitler, Mussolini, and the Japanese. By the end of the 1930s, according to polls by Gallup and *Fortune* magazine, Texas was the most belligerent of the 48 states, and Texans began enlisting in significant numbers. In 1939, for example, 16-year-old Gordon Jones of Livingston fibbed about his age to join the Texas National Guard. The next year, his 36th Division was incorporated into the regular army. After intensive training, the 36th Division invaded Italy in 1943. An artillery blast killed two men beside Private Jones and severely injured his right arm. After five months in a military hospital in North Africa, Jones went AWOL and made his way back to Italy by ship and truck. Rejoining his company outside Rome, he was promoted to sergeant and soon won a Bronze Star in combat. After the war, Jones attended the University of Texas on the GI Bill and later was instrumental in founding the Texas Military Forces Museum at Camp Mabry. (Courtesy of Angie Jones.)

Claire Chennault was born in 1893 in Commerce, later becoming a Texas high school teacher. During World War I, Chennault was commissioned and entered flight service. He was an innovative tactician and wrote a textbook, but conflicts with superiors, as well as deafness, led to enforced retirement in 1936. In 1937, he was employed by Chaing Kai-shek as an advisor for the Chinese Air Force, which was desperately inferior to the aggressive Japanese Air Force. (Courtesy of the National Archives.)

By 1941, Claire Chennault, having obtained 100 P-40 fighter planes, organized and trained the American Volunteer Group (AVG). American pilots and ground crew from U.S. Army and U.S. Navy air forces were recruited at high salaries to challenge Japanese air superiority over China. Pilots were paid as much as $750 per month along with a bonus of $500 for every enemy kill. Piloting the most distinctive aircraft of the war, Chennault's Flying Tigers shot down nearly 300 Japanese planes. (Courtesy of the National Archives.)

Col. David L. "Tex" Hill attended Texas Military Institute and graduated from Austin College. In 1939, he earned his wings as a naval aviator, and two years later, he was recruited by Claire Chennault. Tex Hill became a top ace of the Flying Tigers, shooting down 12 Japanese planes. Joining the U.S. Army Air Force in 1942, he was the first pilot of a P-51 to shoot down a Zero. Five more kills brought his total to 18. Hill died in Texas in 2007 at 92. (Courtesy of the Nimitz Museum.)

Two 18-year-olds await physical exams in San Augustine prior to their acceptance into the armed forces. More than 830,000 Texans, including 12,000 women, donned uniforms before and during the war. (Courtesy of John and Betty Oglesbee.)

Doris "Dorie" Miller was born and raised on a farm near Waco. After war began in Europe in September 1939, nineteen-year-old Dorie enlisted in the U.S. Navy. He was assigned to the USS *West Virginia*, one of eight battleships in the Pacific Fleet, which headquartered in Hawaii at Pearl Harbor. At 6 foot, 3 inches, and 225 pounds, the strapping Texan was a champion service boxer. On Sunday, December 7, 1941, Dorie's fighting instincts would be turned against attackers from the sky. (Courtesy of the Texas Collection, Baylor University, Waco.)

During the early moments of the Japanese air attack on Pearl Harbor, the USS *West Virginia* was struck by seven torpedoes and two bombs, and Capt. Mervyn Bennion was mortally wounded on the bridge. The large man at the right of the bridge may be Dorie Miller, who carried the captain to a sheltered area, then began firing a machine gun. Although Miller had no gunnery training, he said, "I think I got one of those planes." (Courtesy of the National Archives.)

Banner headlines across Texas and the nation proclaimed the Japanese attack on Pearl Harbor. The United States was hurled into the war on Sunday, December 7, 1941, and on Monday morning, Texas men lined up in droves at recruiting stations. Responding to the call to arms as they had for more than a century, Texans represented over 7 percent of the men and women in uniform, even though the Lone Star state had just 5 percent of the American population. (Courtesy of the Dallas *Morning News*.)

Texas senator Tom Connally was chairman of the Senate Foreign Relations Committee from 1941 to 1947 (and again from 1949 to 1953). From this key position, he successfully guided the Lend-Lease Act of 1941 through the legislative process. On December 8, 1941, Senator Connally introduced the resolution for a declaration of war, and at right, he peers over the president's shoulder as FDR signs the act that passed the House, 388-1, and the Senate, 82-0. (Courtesy of the National Archives.)

Two

BASES IN EAST TEXAS

A class of WASPs (Women's Air force Service Pilots) graduates in ceremonies at Avenger Field in Sweetwater. Avenger Field, although not located in the eastern part of the state, was unique among military bases. It was the only all-female training base in America. WASPs and WAFS (Women's Auxiliary Service Ferry Squadron) flew more than 60 million miles during the war, freeing male pilots for combat roles. (Courtesy of Texas Women's University Libraries.)

The stone portals of Gate 5, located 8 miles north of Paris, marked the main entrance at Camp Maxey. With passage of the Selective Service Act in 1940, local officials lobbied for establishment of an army training camp near Paris. The 70,000-acre site was being surveyed when Pearl Harbor was attacked. Activated in July 1942, Camp Maxey had a troop capacity of 45,000, as well as a POW compound for 7,000 prisoners. There was an artillery range, an obstacle course, and a German village. Almost 195,000 soldiers trained at Camp Maxey, and there were 10,300 civilian jobs on base. Area residents housed thousands of dependents, while local women formed the "Maxey Command" to stage dances for soldiers. Deactivated on October 1, 1945, Camp Maxey later became a training center for the Texas National Guard. (Photographs by the author.)

With a pressing need to train vast numbers of pilots and other military air personnel, the Army Air Corps contracted with privately owned flight schools to provide a key step in its training program. Corsicana Field was a training facility of the Air Activities of Texas. Established by local businessmen in 1941 on a 400-acre property 6 miles south of Corsicana, construction included airplane hangars, maintenance facilities, barracks, a mess hall, offices, and a runway 2,000 feet long by 225 feet wide. The 10-week training period included 60 hours of flight instruction and 140 hours of ground school, in addition to physical training. During almost four years of operation, more than 8,000 cadets received primary flight training at Corsicana Field. Several fight instructors were local pilots, and classroom instructors included highly regarded teachers from Corsicana High School. (Both, courtesy of Navarro College.)

Early in 1942, the army established a major medical center in East Texas. Harmon General Hospital was named for Col. David W. Harmon (1880–1940), a medical officer for 36 years. Within a few months, 220 buildings were erected on a 156-acre site just south of Longview. The hospital had facilities for surgery, physical therapy, laboratory analysis, and dental care. There were 2,939 beds and a peak staff of 1,507, including 270 WACS. Later there was a compound for German POWs. (Both, courtesy of Gregg County Historical Society.)

Harmon General Hospital was a self-reliant community. In addition to medical facilities, there were barracks, mess halls, and living quarters for doctors and nurses. There was a bank, post office, theater, gym, chapel, library, post exchange, and laundry. The Garden Club of Longview landscaped the grounds, while local women volunteered as Red Cross Gray Ladies and manned the Red Cross Motor Corps to take patients on outings. The last of 25,000 patients left in December 1945, and on January 20, 1946, Harmon General was deactivated. (Courtesy Gregg County Historical Society.)

In 1942 and 1943, twenty-four German U-boats hunted Allied merchant ships and tankers in the Gulf of Mexico, sinking 56 vessels and damaging another 14. At Hitchcock Naval Air Station, just across West Bay and north of Galveston, a blimp station was established. One of the largest wooden buildings in the world, a hangar measuring 960 feet long, 328 feet wide, and 200 feet tall housed six blimps, which would scour the Gulf for U-boats. (Courtesy of the National Archives.)

After Pearl Harbor, three old forts built to protect Galveston Island were refurbished and modernized. A 100-foot tower was erected at each fort, and antiaircraft guns were installed, along with modern coastal guns, including two 10-inch "disappearing guns" at Fort Crockett (1903). Fort San Jacinto (1901) overlooked the Houston Ship Channel from the eastern end of the island. Fort Travis (1898), positioned to protect the north of Galveston Bay, was garrisoned with 2,500 men during World War II. (Courtesy of the National Archives.)

Fort Crockett, at the west end of Galveston Island, was greatly expanded during World War II. Although no longer a military installation today, many buildings of old Fort Crockett, like the one above, remain in use. In 1943, a total of 650 German POWs were incarcerated at Fort Crockett. There were four main batteries at Fort Crockett, and today the luxurious San Luis Hotel looms above the concrete gun casements at Battery Hoskins, which housed a 12-inch coastal gun. (Photographs by the author.)

During 1942, an infantry replacement training center was established 8 miles northeast of Tyler. Some 2,000 acres of hilly, forested terrain were purchased, and another 13,000 acres were leased. Beginning in December 1942, hundreds of prefab structures were erected at Camp Fannin, while streets were cut through the woods. Trainees began arriving in June 1943. (Photograph by the author.)

As many as 18,000 men at a time underwent training at Camp Fannin to replace troops killed, wounded, or recalled from combat. An estimated 150,000 soldiers were trained at Camp Fannin. There was room for an artillery range, a German POW compound, and a WAC installation. The base created jobs for 3,000 civilian workers and at the end of the war served as a separation center until January 1946. Camp Fannin artifacts are on display at Tyler's Smith County Museum. (Photograph by the author.)

The top-secret Norden bombsight was installed in all B-17 and B-24 bombers. This new device featured a telescopic sight and a mechanical calculator, which computed bomb trajectories, allowing for the plane's speed and altitude. Lenses for the Norden bombsight were made at a nondescript building on Erwin Street in west Tyler, and workers were sworn to secrecy. (Courtesy of the Historic Aviation Museum at Pounds Field, Tyler.)

U.S. Army Air Corps mechanics were vital members of the garrison at each of the 65 air bases in Texas, from Avenger Field of the WASPs to the privately owned Air Activities fields of Texas to the No. 1 British Training School of Terrell to San Antonio's Randolph Field, "the West Point of the Air." (Courtesy of the No. 1 British Flying Training School [BFTS] Museum.)

The No. 1 British Flying Training School from the air was a familiar sight to cadet pilots. Training planes are parked between and beside the hangars, and the two hangars at left still stand today. Pres. Franklin Roosevelt pushed the Lend-Lease Bill through Congress in March 1941, and this facility was built through the Lend-Lease program of aid to nations that opposed Germany and Italy (and soon, Japan). (Courtesy of the No. 1 BFTS Museum.)

As pilot cadets in the United States, British fliers were not officially attached to the Royal Air Force (RAF) prior to Pearl Harbor. Instead, their uniforms bore the BFTS insignia of a British Flying Training School. The number 1 indicates that the Terrell facility was the first British Flying Training School in America. (Courtesy of the No. 1 BFTS Museum.)

RAF pilot cadets were transported by ship from England to Canada. The first cadets arrived in 1941, before the United States entered the war. The cadets changed to civilian clothes before traveling incognito by train across the United States to Terrell, Texas. After arriving at the new training field, the cadets were issued BFTS uniforms. (Courtesy of the No. 1 BFTS Museum.)

The Operations and Flight Control building was the nerve center for the No. 1 British Flying Training School in Terrell. RAF cadets and their instructors are walking in their flight suits toward parked planes. (Courtesy of the No. 1 BFTS Museum.)

BFTS cadets assemble in front of the flagpole. The two buildings behind them are barracks, and behind each barracks is a classroom building. Beyond the classroom building at left stands the mess hall, and at the end of the sidewalk is the civilian administration building. (Courtesy of the No. 1 BFTS Museum.)

Cadet pilots spent far more time in the classroom than in the air. Ground-school courses included meteorology, mathematics, navigation, maps, airplane engines, and airplane identification. These cadets are studying navigation with a naviscope. (Courtesy of the No. 1 BFTS Museum.)

The Link Trainer was a flight simulator that was a key element to pilot preparation at all training fields. A civilian instructor sits at the simulation controls of the Link Trainer. (Courtesy of the No. 1 BFTS Museum.)

LINK TRAINER OFFICE

The Link Training Group poses for a photograph outside the Link Trainer Office. These civilian employees from Terrell wore BFTS uniforms. (Courtesy of the No. 1 BFTS Museum.)

In 1938, North American Aviation began producing an early series of the AT-6 Advanced Fighter Trainer for England and Canada. By 1941, a plant in Dallas was producing the AT-6 for Britain, China, and Latin American countries, as well as for the U.S. military. More than 4,000 were manufactured in Dallas, and the AT-6 began to be called the "Texan" (note "TEX" on the lettering of this AT-6). Upon completion, each AT-6 was flown, usually by a WASP, to its training base. (Courtesy of the Lone Star Flight Museum.)

The No. 1 British Flying Training School in Terrell used the AT-6 to train future RAF pilots. These AT-6s are parked in front of the control tower at Terrell's BFTS base. (Courtesy of the No. 1 BFTS Museum.)

Most cadet pilots began flight training in biplanes, then progressed to the AT-6. The AT-6 was comparable in power and maneuverability to a fighter plane, although because of the wartime shortage of metal, these trainers were built of plywood. More than 100,000 fighter pilots finished their training in "the Pilot Maker." (Courtesy of the No. 1 BFTS Museum.)

Pilot cadets trained at sighting guns at other planes with a gun camera in the AT-6. The U.S. Navy began ordering a version called the SNJ, which was equipped with landing-gear hooks for landing on an aircraft carrier. (Courtesy of the No. 1 BFTS Museum.)

A favorite sport of the English lads at No. 1 BFTS was soccer. A victorious team poses proudly with its trophy, and the trophy is part of the rich collection at the No. 1 British Flying Training Museum. (Both, courtesy of the No. 1 BFTS Museum.)

BFTS cadets assemble at Terrell's Oakland Memorial Cemetery for the graveside services of a fellow cadet pilot. Out of more than 1,400 RAF cadets (and 138 U.S. pilots) who earned their wings at No. 1 BFTS, 19 were killed in training, 1 died of natural causes, and 3 flight instructors were also killed. (Courtesy of the No. 1 BFTS Museum.)

The English cadet pilots who died at No. 1 BFTS during the war were interred in a special plat at Oakland Memorial Cemetery in the west end of Terrell. (Photograph by the author.)

Henry Madgwick spent his 21st birthday while training at No. 1 BFTS, and he is pointing to himself in the Course 24 photograph. Cadets were permitted to go into town on Wednesday evenings and Saturdays and Sundays, and they were often hosted by ladies of the Terrell War Relief Society. The 28-week training course was enough time for romances to develop. After the war, several Terrell women traveled to England for marriage, and Henry and Tonell Madgwick returned to Texas to make their home. Henry is now active at the BFTS Museum. (Courtesy of the No. 1 BFTS Museum.)

Three

TEXAS HEROES

Audie Leon Murphy was born in
Hunt County in 1924 into a large
family of sharecroppers. Young
Audie hunted the woods with a
single-shot .22 rifle, becoming a
crack shot and developing a feel
for the terrain. At 18, he enlisted
in the army. He fought with
courage and skill in Sicily, Italy,
France, and Germany, suffering
three wounds and taking part
in amphibious assaults in Sicily
and southern France. The most
decorated American soldier
of World War II, Murphy was
presented 33 awards, including
every medal the United States
offers for valor—two of them twice.
(Courtesy of the Audie Murphy/
American Cotton Museum.)

Awarded a battlefield commission, 2nd Lt. Audie Murphy won the Medal of Honor during an action near Holtzwihr, France, on January 26, 1945. Murphy's Company B was attacked by six tanks and a large infantry force. Ordering his men to return to prepared positions in nearby woods, Lieutenant Murphy remained forward while giving fire directions to artillery by telephone. Many advancing Germans halted, but the enemy tanks lumbered toward his position. Murphy climbed on a burning tank destroyer, which had been disabled by a shell and was in danger of blowing up, but Murphy manned the .50-caliber machine gun and turned the attack, mowing down one enemy squad that crept within 10 yards of him. Exposed atop the destroyer, he was wounded in the leg but killed or wounded 50 Germans. Refusing medical attention, Murphy organized a counterattack against the retreating Germans. (Both, courtesy of the Audie Murphy/American Cotton Museum.)

Truman Kimbro from Madisonville was a member of the 2nd Engineer Battalion of the 2nd Engineer Division. Acting as scout, he led a squad assigned to mine crossroads in Belgium. But the position was commanded by an enemy tank and at least 20 German soldiers. After the squad was thrown back three times, Kimbro crawled out alone, laden with mines. Although severely wounded, he laid the mines, then was riddled by machine-gun fire. Kimbro was awarded the Medal of Honor posthumously. (From *The Medal of Honor*.)

In Burma on February 2, 1945, 1st Lt. Jack Knight led his company in an assault against a nest of Japanese pillboxes. He single-handedly knocked out two pillboxes and killed the occupants of several foxholes. While attacking a third pillbox, he was struck and blinded by a third grenade, but he continued to move forward with his men until he was mortally wounded. Lieutenant Knight was awarded a Medal of Honor. (From *The Medal of Honor*.)

On January 6, 1944, Col. Neal Kearby of Wichita Falls volunteered to lead four fighter planes to reconnoiter a Japanese base near Wewak in New Guinea. Over Wewak, Kearby sighted a lone enemy fighter and sent it flaming into the sea. Then he led his little squadron against a flight of 12 bombers and more than 30 fighters. Kearby quickly shot down three planes before pursuing and destroying two fighters on the tail of one of his planes. The audacious attack and six kills resulted in a Medal of Honor. (From *The Medal of Honor.*)

1st Lt. Jack Mathis was awarded the Medal of Honor for "undaunted bravery" during a bombing run over Vegesack, Germany, on March 18, 1943. The lead bombardier of the squadron, Lieutenant Mathis was knocked off his Norden bombsight during the approach to the target. Critically wounded by antiaircraft fire, Mathis suffered a gaping hole in his side and a shattered right arm, but he crawled back to the bombsight, released his load, then died at his post. (From *The Medal of Honor.*)

On November 27, 1944, Sgt. Marcario Garcia single-handedly assaulted two machine-gun emplacements near Grossau, Germany, earning a Medal of Honor for "conspicuous heroism" and "complete disregard for his personal safety." His company was pinned down by machine-gun fire then subjected to a concentrated artillery and mortar barrage. Although painfully wounded, Sergeant Garcia crawled forward alone until he could hurl grenades into a machine-gun emplacement. He charged the position, killing three German soldiers with his rifle. When a second machine gun opened fire, Sergeant Garcia stormed the position, destroying the gun, killing three more soldiers, and capturing four of the enemy. He continued to fight until his unit's objective was achieved, only then permitting himself to be removed for medical treatment. (From *The Medal of Honor*.)

According to *The Medal of Honor*, "By his outstanding skill with his weapons, gallant determination to destroy the enemy, and heroic courage in the face of tremendous odds," Pvt. Cleto Rodriguez of San Marcos earned the Medal of Honor for two gallant actions during the Battle of Manila. On November 1, 1945, his platoon was halted while attacking the Paco Railroad Station. On their own initiative, Rodriguez and a comrade moved to an advanced position and, during the next hour, killed 35 enemy soldiers and wounded many more. Advancing again, they killed more than 40. Covered by his comrade, Rodriguez charged a 20mm gun position, killing seven Japanese while wrecking the 20mm gun and a machine gun. While withdrawing, Rodriguez's comrade was slain. Two days later, Rodriguez "single-handedly killed six Japanese and destroyed a well-placed 20mm gun." (From *The Medal of Honor*.)

Praha was a Czech-Texan community in Fayette County with a population estimated at 100. Tragically, nine sons of Praha were killed in action during a one-year period beginning February 1944. In North Africa, Pfc. Robert Bohnslav was the first to die. In France, Pfc. Rudolph Bart fell 10 days after D-Day. Four were killed in July 1944: in France, Sgt. George Pavlicek and Pvt. Jerry Vaculik; in Italy, Pvt. Alvye Ral; in the Philippines, Pvt. Joseph Lea. In September 1944, Pvt. Eddie Sbrusch was lost at sea in the Pacific and Pfc. Edward Marek was killed in action on Pelilieu Island. And in February 1945, Pfc. Anton Kresh Jr. died in the Philippines. These brave men are pictured on a granite monument at the entrance to the parish cemetery behind beautiful St. Mary's Catholic Church. The monument also honors chaplain Marcus Valenta, a Pearl Harbor survivor. Three small chapels around the church also honor fallen men. (Photographs by the author.)

In April 1945, 1st Lt. James A. Robinson Jr. was attached to Company A of the 253rd Infantry as a field artillery forward observer. Near Untergriesheim, Germany, on April 6, the company engaged in combat over open terrain. After eight hours of desperate fighting, the commanding officer and most other lead personnel were out of action. Lieutenant Robinson organized the 23 uninjured men and a few walking wounded, then led a charge through intense fire. At point-blank range, using his rifle and a .45-automatic pistol, he killed 10 Germans in foxholes. Next he led his makeshift assault force into the town of Kressbach. Wounded in the throat by a shell fragment, he pressed the attack until the town was secured. No longer able to speak and bleeding profusely, Lieutenant Robinson walked 2 miles to an aid station, where he died. He was awarded a Medal of Honor posthumously. (From *The Medal of Honor*.)

Near Prumzerly, Germany, on February 27, 1945, Company B of the 301st Engineer Combat Battalion was clearing mines from a road. Pvt. Herman Wallace stepped on a concealed antipersonnel mine, which, if he leaped aside, would be hurled above ground to explode and spray his comrades with fragments. Wallace's best chance for survival was to fall prone, but selflessly he placed his other foot on the mine to keep it in the ground. Wallace sacrificed his life for his comrades, and he was posthumously awarded the Medal of Honor. (From *The Medal of Honor*.)

During the Allied push to establish a bridgehead across the Po River in Italy, Lt. Raymond Knight volunteered to lead an air attack against nearby air bases. These bases were well-defended, but the Texan intended to destroy camouflaged aircraft that could threaten the advance. On April 24 and 25, he led three low-level attacks, destroying 24 enemy aircraft. On the third attack, his P-47 Thunderbolt was badly damaged, and he crashed while trying to return. Lieutenant Knight was awarded a Medal of Honor posthumously. (From *The Medal of Honor*.)

Gen. Dwight D. "Ike" Eisenhower, supreme commander of Allied Forces in Europe, was born in 1890 in Denison, Texas. Ike was the only one of six Eisenhower sons born in Texas, and before his first birthday the family returned to Kansas. Raised in Abilene, Ike graduated from West Point in 1915. Lieutenant Eisenhower's first post was at Fort Sam Houston in San Antonio, where he met and courted his future bride, Mamie Doud of Denver, Colorado. In June 1941, Colonel Eisenhower returned to Fort Sam Houston as chief of staff to the commander of III Corps, Gen. Walter Krueger. Ike was promoted to brigadier general in September 1941, following brilliant leadership of large-scale field maneuvers. Summoned from Texas to Washington after Pearl Harbor, within a year General Eisenhower led the invasions of North Africa, Sicily, and Italy, as well as the massive D-Day assault at Normandy. He ended the war a five-star general and, in 1952, won the first of two terms as president. (Both, courtesy of the National Archives.)

A display of the Medal of Honor winners from Texas stands in the basement of the Texas State Capitol. The Congressional Medal of Honor originated during the Civil War. More than 70 Texans have earned the medal, half of them during World War II. Beneath each photograph is a description of the recipient and of his exploits. Pictured at right is one of the World War II panels. (Photograph by the author.)

Walton H. Walker was born in 1889 in Belton. He attended Wedemeyer Military Academy in his home town and Virginia Military Institute. A 1912 graduate of West Point, he saw combat in World War I, and in World War II, General Walker commanded the IV Armored Corps and XX Corps under hard-driving Gen. George Patton (left, with Walker at his side). Walker ended the war a major general, and as lieutenant general, he was killed in Korea in 1950. (Courtesy of the National Archives.)

"It would have never crossed my mind to command an army of women," said Col. Oveta Culp Hobby. "I never did learn to salute properly." Colonel Hobby, wife of former Texas governor William P. Hobby, was a woman of high intelligence and impressive accomplishment. The Hobbys owned and operated the *Houston Post* and KPRC Radio, and on the eve of war, Oveta was in Washington dealing with the FCC. After Congress established the first peacetime draft, women by the tens of thousands wrote to Washington asking how they could serve their country. Gen. George C. Marshall and Secretary of War Henry Stimson asked Oveta Hobby to study the English and French women's armies and to list army tasks that could be performed by women. After Pearl Harbor, General Marshall asked her to organize and command the Women's Army Auxiliary Corps (WAAC) with the rank of colonel. Colonel Hobby is pictured at left, and below is WAAC recruit Pat Costello of Uvalde. (Both, courtesy of Texas Women's University Libraries.)

Colonel Hobby, second from left, was present when Charity Adams Earley (second from right) was presented her WAAC commission. Earley was the first African American woman to receive an army commission. Colonel Hobby traveled constantly, fulfilling a heavy speaking schedule and visiting WAAC bases. Under her leadership, WAACs assumed 239 types of jobs, working in postal battalions, vehicle maintenance, photograph and map departments, and clerical positions, thus freeing thousands of soldiers for martial duties. In 1943, this auxiliary force was accepted into the army as the Women's Army Corps (WAC), and by the next year, commanders in every theater had requested a total of 600,000 WACs. The peak strength was about 100,000 officers and enlisted women, with more than 17,000 WACS serving overseas. Clad in fatigues, the WAC group at right, including Texan Pat Costello, is on duty in the Pacific. (Both, courtesy of Texas Women's University Libraries.)

Texas was the training center for the Women's Airforce Service Pilots (WASP). Avenger Field in Sweetwater was the only all-female training base in the United States. More than 25,000 women pilots applied to become WASPs and flew as an auxiliary outfit that had no official military connection. WASP recruits had to pay their own way to Avenger Field, and at first there were no uniforms or even cot mattresses, but the WASPs overcame all obstacles and flew more than 60 million miles in every type of U.S. plane—trainers, fighters, bombers, and transport craft. WASPS ferried planes across long distances, tested experimental and repaired aircraft, towed targets for ground-to-air and air-to-air firing practice, and accompanied cadet pilots in the air. Thirty-eight WASP pilots were killed while flying for their country. (Both, courtesy of Texas Women's University Libraries.)

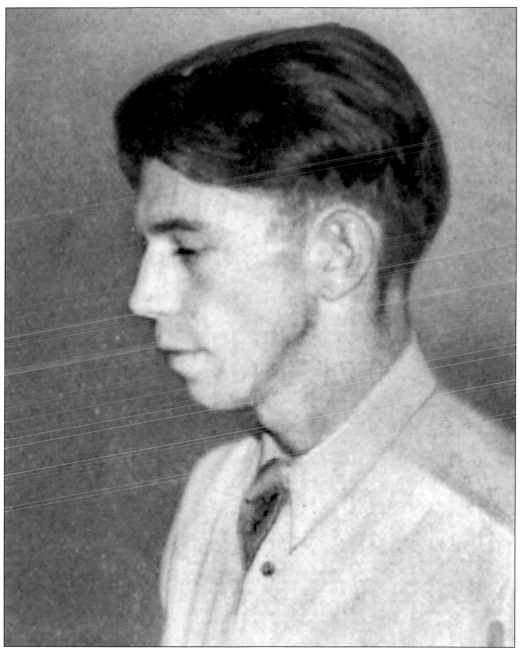

Sgt. Forrest Everheart led a platoon in Company H of the 359th Infantry in the 90th Division. Before dawn on November 12, 1944, Sergeant Everheart's outnumbered and outgunned platoon bore the brunt of an enemy counterattack against an American bridgehead across the Moselle River. When German tanks and self-propelled guns penetrated the left flank of his position, Sergeant Everheart ran 400 yards under fire to reinforce the sole remaining machine gunner. As infantrymen swarmed close to the position, he charged the attackers and threw grenades until the Germans retreated, leaving 30 dead. Then Everheart ran back across the fire-swept terrain to direct the men defending his right flank. Again he engaged in a hand-grenade duel, resulting in 20 enemy dead and a German withdrawal. (From *The Medal of Honor*.)

Pfc. Ralph Richards, a graduate of Emhouse High School, trained at Camp Fannin in Tyler and later became part of Patton's Third Army during the famous drive into Germany. At Uerdingen, the Rhine River was spanned by the enormous Adolph Hitler Autobahn Bridge. When U.S. troops reached the bridge, a battle exploded with Germans on the east flank, and the four-lane bridge was damaged. Before dawn on March 4, 1945, Private Richards joined a seven-man patrol assigned to determine if the bridge could be crossed. In a driving rainstorm and with fierce crossfire beneath them, Richards and his comrades crossed the bridge. About 300 yards from the east end, they had to step down from a crater onto a narrow I-beam and shuffle across the girder. Soon finding further damage, and with one man wounded, they returned under fire. Moments later, the bridge detonated and collapsed. All seven men were awarded the Silver Star. (Both, courtesy of Albert Richards.)

A strapping farm boy, Jack Lummus was a star football and baseball player at Ennis High School. He attended Texas Military Institute and Baylor University as a scholarship athlete. At Baylor he was an All–Southwest Conference center fielder for three years, and in football, he was an honorable mention All-American end. In 1941, he played minor league baseball for the Wichita Falls Spudders, and that fall, he joined the NFL with the New York Giants. Early in 1942, Lummus enlisted in the U.S. Marine Corps and earned a commission. On February 19, 1945, First Lieutenant Lummus led a platoon ashore in the first wave at Iwo Jima. Three weeks later, when his men were pinned down by heavy fire, he single-handedly wiped out three pillbox positions, ignoring wounds from two grenades. But his legs were blown off by a land mine, and he said to the surgeon at the aid station, "Well, Doc, the New York Giants lost a mighty good end today." Lummus died during surgery, and he was posthumously awarded the Medal of Honor. (Author's collection.)

Sgt. Lucian Adams of Port Arthur earned the Medal of Honor with a lone assault of a strong German position in the Mortagne Forest. Sergeant Adams's company was assigned to drive through the forest and reopen supply lines to the isolated 3rd Battalion of the 3rd Infantry Division. Advancing into the forest, the company was halted by fire from three machine guns, which killed three and wounded six more. Firing a Browning Automatic Rifle (BAR) from his hip, Sergeant Adams darted from tree to tree. Ten yards from the first machine gun, he killed a gunner with a grenade and a rifleman with a burst from his BAR. Charging the second machine gun, he killed the gunner with another hand grenade and forced two riflemen to surrender. Plunging deeper into the woods, he killed five more men, then dispatched the last machine gunner with his BAR. Sergeant Adams single-handedly killed nine men and cleared the woods to reopen the supply line. (From *The Medal of Honor*.)

During the drive into Germany, Sgt. Gordon Darnell of Carthage was in charge of three 60mm mortar squads in a weapons platoon. On the night of December 5, 1944, his position was infiltrated by enemy soldiers, but Sergeant Darnell and a companion emerged from their foxhole and, with rifles and hand grenades, killed three Germans, wounded two, and routed the others. Sergeant Darnell received the Bronze Star, as well as the Purple Heart for wounds received in action on April 23, 1945. (Courtesy Drew Darnell.)

Born and raised on a farm in Hemphill County, Cpl. Ordria Gipson was one of many Texas fighting men who gravitated to the U.S. Marines. He experienced vicious combat in Guam, Bougainville, and Iwo Jima, earning a Bronze Star and Purple Heart. Returning to East Texas after the war, he married Louise Williams of Garrison. There he became the town barber, a deacon of the First Baptist Church, and the father of three children. (Courtesy of Faye Gipson Frasier.)

Born at Fort Sam Houston, Robert G. Cole was a lieutenant colonel of the 101st Airborne Division, which parachuted into France the night before the D-Day invasion. Five days later, on June 11, 1944, Lieutenant Colonel Cole was leading his battalion toward Carentan when the command was pinned down by artillery, mortar, machine gun, and rifle fire. Seeing his men suffering heavy casualties, Lieutenant Colonel Cole ordered a bayonet charge. Cole led the charge through a hail of fire and overran the enemy position. "His heroic and valiant action in so inspiring his men resulted in the complete establishment of our bridgehead across the Douve River," read his Medal of Honor citation. (From *The Medal of Honor.*)

Four

TEXAS AGGIES AT WAR

The Agricultural and Mechanical College of Texas was an all-male military school that provided 20,229 fighting men during World War II. Texas A&M produced 14,123 officers, more than any other college or university, including the U.S. Military Academy at West Point. Aggies fought on every front and played prominent roles in one battle after another. (Courtesy of Texas A&M.)

The corps of cadets was instructed in military subjects by regular army officers. In 1935, the Department of Military Science and Tactics was directed by Lt. Col. A. R. Emery, standing in the center of the front row. Emery held a faculty position as professor of military science and tactics, and his instructors included five first lieutenants, five captains, four majors, and another lieutenant colonel, as well as about 40 army non-commissioned officers. (Courtesy of Texas A&M.)

The corps of cadets was organized into companies and battalions, with student staff officers. Above is the 1935 Headquarters Battery of the 1st Battalion of Field Artillery. By 1940, with the United States building up for a war effort, there were more than 6,000 cadets in the corps. (Courtesy of Texas A&M.)

Raymond L. Murray of Nixon was commandant of the corps infantry regiment during his senior year (1934–1935), graduating with a U.S. Marine commission. In World War II Lieutenant Colonel Murray won a Silver Star during brutal combat at Guadalcanal and another Silver Star during the murderous invasion of Tarawa. Murray was wounded while defending battalion headquarters at Saipan, but he continued to direct the action, earning the U.S. Navy Cross. During the Korean War, he fought brilliantly and was awarded the Distinguished Service Cross. Former cadet Murray ended his notable career as a major general in the U.S. Marine Corps. (Courtesy of Texas A&M.)

During the 1930s, every student at A&M was required to be a member of the corps for at least his freshman and sophomore years. Aggies who remained in the corps as juniors and seniors were awarded army commissions upon graduation, along with their baccalaureate degrees. Each summer, members of the corps trained at federal military installations, such as these Aggies at Camp Bullis, 17 miles northwest of Fort Sam Houston in San Antonio. (Courtesy of Texas A&M.)

Aggies in summer training at Camp Bullis handled weapons from field artillery to the 1911 Colt .45 automatic, the superb sidearm of the American military. (Courtesy of Texas A&M.)

Col. George L. Moore (class of 1908), a veteran of World War I, was assigned to command the corps of cadets in 1937. He modernized and strengthened the corps before being transferred in 1940. Ordered to a third tour of duty in the Philippines, Moore brought a number of young officers from A&M with him. Promoted to brigadier general early in 1941, he was the first Aggie to reach flag rank. During the five-month siege of Bataan and Corregidor at the beginning of the war, Gen. Douglas MacArthur was ordered to remove himself to Australia. Gen. Jonathan Wainwright was left in overall command, while General Moore commanded all infantry and U.S. Marine forces. An overwhelming Japanese assault forced the starving defenders to surrender on May 6, 1942. (Courtesy of Texas A&M.)

At Texas A&M, Tom Dooley of McKinney, photographed at left in his senior boots, was a yell leader and a member of the Ross Volunteers. At graduation in 1935, Dooley was commissioned into the army. By December 1941, he was a major, serving as aide-de-camp to Jonathan Wainwright in the Philippines. Wainwright was forced to surrender his force at Corregidor, but Dooley survived the long internment and was chosen to witness the Japanese surrender aboard the USS *Missouri*. (Courtesy of Texas A&M.)

Artifacts from Corregidor are displayed at the Corps of Cadets Center on the A&M campus. (Photograph by the author.)

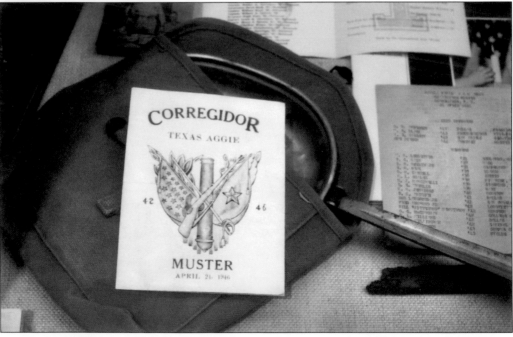

The first American counterattack against the islands of Japan was led by Col. James Doolittle. The bombing raid on Tokyo was executed by 16 twin-engine B-25s. The five-man crews were specially trained to take off from an aircraft carrier, and among the 80 fliers were 5 Aggies. Doolittle's copilot was Lt. James M. Parker (class of 1941) of Houston. In the top photograph, Doolittle is at the front left, and beside him in front is Lieutenant Parker. Doolittle's second-in-command, Maj. Jack Higler of Sherman, piloted plane No. 14 and is shown below (second from left) with his crew. Other Aggies on the Tokyo raid were three pilots: Lt. William M. Fitzhugh (class of 1936), Lt. Glen C. Roloson (class of 1940), and Lt. Robert M. Gray (class of 1941). The flight of B-25s left the carrier *Hornet* on April 18, 1942, and the bombing of Tokyo was an enormous morale boost to the American people. (Both, courtesy of the National Archives.)

The war was only a few months old when Capt. James Connally, cousin of Sen. Tom Connally, led a flight of five planes from Java to Mindanao. Sinking a Japanese freighter en route, the planes landed on Mindanao to rescue 23 stranded American pilots. Connally received the Distinguished Flying Cross for leading the mission, but later in the war, he was killed in action over Yokohama. In his honor, the Waco Army Air Field was renamed James Connally Air Force Base in 1949. (Courtesy of Texas A&M.)

Ens. George Gay (class of 1940) from Waco piloted a Douglas Devastator torpedo bomber with Torpedo Squadron 8 aboard the carrier *Hornet*. During the Battle of Midway, a spectacular turning point for U.S. forces in the Pacific, Ensign Gay was the only survivor of his squadron. Wounded and shot down in the midst of the enemy fleet, he clung to a flotation device and witnessed the destruction of three Japanese carriers. The fleet departed, and after 30 hours in the sea, he was rescued by a Navy PBY seaplane. (Courtesy of Texas A&M.)

Maj. Horace S. Carswell Jr. piloted a B-24 bomber in a single-plane strike against a Japanese convoy in the South China Sea on the night of October 26, 1944. A low-altitude bombing run resulted in two direct hits on a tanker, but the B-24 was riddled with antiaircraft fire. Two engines were knocked out, a third was damaged, the hydraulic system was crippled, the copilot was wounded, and the parachute of one crew member was badly torn. The crippled bomber plunged toward the sea, "but by magnificent display of flying skill," Carswell leveled off and headed for the China coast. Over land, the third engine failed, and Carswell ordered his men to bail out. Sticking with the crew member whose parachute was useless, Carswell tried to execute a crash landing, but the B-24 slammed into a mountainside and burned. Major Carswell was posthumously awarded a Medal of Honor, and in 1949, Fort Worth's Tarrant Field was renamed after him. (From *The Medal of Honor.*)

On May 23, 1944, Lt. Thomas W. Fowler (class of 1943), a tank officer, found himself on foot during a full-scale armored-infantry battle near Carano, Italy. He encountered two disorganized infantry platoons held up by a minefield. Advancing into the minefield, Fowler cleared a 75-yard path by lifting the mines out of the ground by hand. Returning to the two platoons, he led them through the minefield one squad at a time before leading two tanks through the field. Next he led an advance, acting as scout 300 yards in front, where he killed or captured several enemy soldiers in foxholes. As his two platoons retreated before a counterattack, the lieutenant braved enemy fire to render first aid to nine wounded GIs. Ten days after this Medal of Honor exploit, Lieutenant Fowler was killed when the Fifth Army marched toward Rome. Fowler's medal is on display at A&M. (Both, courtesy of Texas A&M.)

Although a member of the Aggie class of 1943, Lloyd Hughes volunteered for the Air Corps early in the war. On August 1, 1943, Lieutenant Hughes was the pilot of a B-24 during the massive bombing raid on the Ploesti oil refinery. With his plane struck by antiaircraft fire and badly leaking gasoline, Lieutenant Hughes carried out his bombing run through the blazing refinery. His plane ignited, but Hughes crash-landed, losing his life while saving most of his crew. He was posthumously awarded the Medal of Honor. (Courtesy of Texas A&M.)

Joe Routt (class of 1937) was a ferocious lineman who became A&M's first two-time All-American. As a combat officer in Europe, he led his men with the same aggressiveness he displayed on the gridiron. But during the Battle of the Bulge late in 1944, Captain Routt was killed in action. Two other All-Americans and stars of the 1939 National Championship team, Jarrin' John Kimbrough and Marshall Robnett, also fought in Europe. (Courtesy of Texas A&M.)

Sgt. George Keathley was part of an assault at Mount Altuzzo, Italy, on September 14, 1944. All of the officers and noncoms of the 2nd and 3rd platoons were casualties except for Sergeant Keathley, and only 20 men remained unwounded. Assuming command of these soldiers, Sergeant Keathley crawled under fire from casualty to casualty, administering first aid and collecting badly needed ammunition and grenades. Three German counterattacks were thrown back, but the fourth was launched by two companies against both flanks as well as the front of Keathley's beleaguered position. A grenade explosion inflicted a mortal wound, but Keathley ignored his injury. Removing his hand from his wound, the sergeant stood up and shot an oncoming German soldier. For 15 minutes, he continued to fire and shout orders. As friendly artillery drove off the Germans, Keathley dropped dead. He was awarded a Medal of Honor posthumously. (Courtesy of Texas A&M.)

VALOR

LT. TURNEY W. LEONARD
'42

During a three-day period, November 4–6, 1944, First Lt. Turney Leonard (1942) from Dallas commanded a tank destroyer company throughout a large-scale engagement at Kommerscheidt, Germany. Leonard repeatedly exposed himself, dismounting from his tank destroyer to direct fire and going on solitary reconnaissance missions. When fired upon by a machine gun, he advanced alone and wiped out the emplacement with hand grenades and a Thompson submachine gun. Although wounded early in the battle, he continued to direct fire from his advanced position until an artillery shell took off his lower arm. Tying a tourniquet around his arm, he headed back to an aid station but was never seen again. Lieutenant Leonard was awarded a Medal of Honor posthumously. (Courtesy of Texas A&M.)

Before dawn on March 3, 1945, on the broken terrain of Iwo Jima, Japanese soldiers infiltrated the position of a U.S. Marine assault team led by Sgt. William Harrell. Alertly, Sergeant Harrell killed two of the enemy with his M-1 carbine, but a grenade explosion took off his left hand and broke his thigh. Charged by a Japanese officer brandishing a sword, Harrell pulled his .45 automatic. He killed the officer, then shot two more enemy soldiers. With a live grenade near his head, Harrell shoved it toward another Japanese who was killed by the blast. But Harrell lost his other hand. At dawn, medics pulled Harrell from a pile of 12 dead Japanese soldiers. He survived and was presented the Medal of Honor by Pres. Harry Truman. (Courtesy of Texas A&M.)

VALOR

LT. ELI L. WHITELEY
'41

On December 27, 1944, First Lt. Eli Whiteley led his platoon in savage house-to-house fighting in the fortress town of Sigolsheim, France. Although severely wounded in the arm and shoulder, he charged into a home and killed its 2 defenders. Hurling grenades, he stormed into the next house, killing 2 and capturing 11 Germans. Wedging his Thompson submachine gun under his uninjured arm, he directed bazooka fire, which blasted apart the wall of another house, then charged through the gap. Whiteley killed 5 more Germans and forced 12 to surrender. Emerging into the street, he was again wounded. With one eye pierced by a shell fragment, Whiteley continued to lead his platoon until forcibly evacuated. Despite painful wounds, he killed 9 Germans and captured 23 more, earning the Medal of Honor. (From *The Medal of Honor*.)

Lt. Col. Earl Rudder (class of 1932) commanded the 2nd Ranger Battalion during the D-Day invasion of Normandy. Rudder's Rangers were assigned to scale the 100-foot cliffs of Pointe du Hoc and destroy six 155mm enemy guns. Germans leaned over the cliff top to fire automatic weapons and toss grenades at Rangers clambering up rope ladders. The Rangers suffered 50 percent casualties, including a twice-wounded Rudder. Below, the arrow indicates Rudder with his Rangers. Promoted to full colonel, Rudder led the 109th Infantry Regiment in crucial combat at the Battle of the Bulge. Rudder remained in the U.S. Army National Guard, rising to the rank of major general. In 1959, he became president of Texas A&M, where he remains a legendary figure. There is a prominent statue of President Rudder on the campus, and Rudder's Rangers form an elite unit in the corps of cadets. (Both, courtesy of Texas A&M.)

Capt. Olin E. "Tiger" Teague (class of 1932) participated in the D-Day invasion on June 6, 1944. During the next six months, he was wounded six times while earning three Silver Stars, three Bronze Stars, and numerous other citations. A final wound cost him part of his left leg. In 1946, Teague (second from left) was on the speakers' platform with General Eisenhower as 15,000 Aggies assembled at Kyle Field to honor the 900 men from A&M who gave their lives. That same year, Teague won election to Congress, where he became a champion of veterans' rights. (Courtesy of Texas A&M.)

A noted engineering school, Texas A&M fielded an Engineer Battalion within the corps, and during the war, Aggies were key members of engineer units on all fronts. Above are 10 Aggies of the 189th Engineer Regiment on Shemya Island in the Aleutians in 1943. (Courtesy of Texas A&M.)

"We fought the hell out of them," exulted Capt. James F. Hollingsworth (class of 1940) after battling German armored units in the North African campaign. Captain Hollingsworth next fought in Sicily before participating in the Normandy invasion. During the Battle of the Bulge, Major Hollingsworth commanded the 2nd Battalion of the 67th Armored Regiment, 2nd Armored Division. His combat career continued in Korea and Vietnam, where he led as a lieutenant general. With four Silver Stars, four Bronze Stars, six Purple Hearts, three Distinguished Service Crosses, three Distinguished Flying Crosses, and numerous other medals, Hollingsworth became the most decorated Aggie general. A statue of General Hollingsworth stands proudly on the Aggie quadrangle at A&M, adorned with "79er," his famous call sign in Vietnam. (Photograph by the author.)

Bugle calls signaled reveille, meals, classes, and lights out. The corps bugler inserted his bugle inside a megaphone, which carried the calls across the campus. The megaphone today is mounted on the corps quadrangle. (Photograph by Karon O'Neal, class of 1983.)

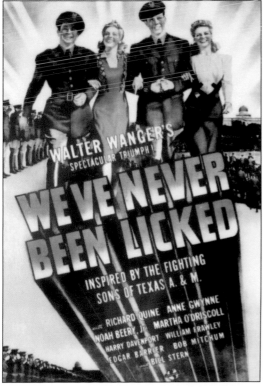

In November 1942, a Hollywood film crew and cast were conspicuous on the A&M campus. Director Walter Wanger lensed scenes for a patriotic movie "inspired by the Fighting Sons of Texas A&M." Future star Robert Mitchum played a cadet in the corps, and so did popular character actor Noah Berry Jr. Set on campus and in the Pacific early in the war, *We've Never Been Licked* helped popularize the image of the Fightin' Texas Aggies. (Courtesy of Texas A&M.)

With the 11,000 defenders of Corregidor reduced to starvation rations and under constant bombardment, Maj. Tom Dooley compiled a roster of 25 Aggies on San Jacinto Day/Aggie Muster Day, April 21, 1942. (12 of the 25 survived their long and difficult internment.) This muster call was included in a *United Press* story about Corregidor, creating the impression that besieged Aggies somehow gathered on April 21 to drink toasts of water to the heroes of San Jacinto, sing A&M songs, and exchange tales of their college days. The story of Aggie Muster on Corregidor quickly gained legendary status, and on battlefronts throughout the remainder of the war, Aggie Musters were held on April 21. On April 21, 1946, Aggies in uniform mustered on Corregidor to pay tribute to the besieged heroes of 1942. (Courtesy of Texas A&M.)

Five

THE T-PATCH DIVISION

Members of the 36th Division wore the T-Patch. When the 36th Division was federalized in 1917, most of the men were Texas National Guard troops, inspiring the nickname "Texas Division," also known as "the Texas Army." The 36th Division experienced heavy combat in 1918. The 36th Division again was federalized on November 25, 1940, with 12,526 men assembling for training at Camp Bowie in Brown County. By the time the United States entered the war, the 36th Division had trained for a year, and a great many experienced Texan noncoms were transferred to newly formed divisions. Soon less than half of T-Patchers were from the Lone Star state, but the 36th Division retained its Texas identity. (Photograph by the author.)

The 36th Division received its baptism of fire on September 9, 1943, landing on the sandy shores of Salerno, Italy. Commanded by Maj. Gen. Fred L. Walker, the 36th became the first American division to invade continental Europe. There had been no preceding naval or air bombardment. German artillery fire was heavy, and planes flew in to strafe the breaches. Armored counterattacks threatened to drive the invaders into the sea. But T-Patchers battled back desperately: a 105mm firing point-blank destroyed five tanks and turned back the other eight, while bazooka teams held the flanks. The 36th Division suffered 1,900 casualties but began to struggle inland. (Both, courtesy of the Texas Military Forces Museum at Camp Mabry, Austin.)

Medal of Honor winner Jim Logan, from McNeil and, after the war, Kilgore, often is called the "second most decorated soldier of World War II." Sergeant Logan was part of the first wave when the 36th Division landed at Salerno. After advancing 800 yards, Logan's company fell under heavy fire from Germans behind a rock wall. Sprinting 200 yards under machine-gun fire, Logan killed three Germans then hurdled the wall and shot the machine gunners. Turning the machine gun on the Germans, he routed his attackers and captured a retreating enemy officer and a private. Later in the morning, he advanced 150 yards under fire from a sniper concealed in a house. Logan shot the lock off the door, kicked it in, and killed the sniper. (From *The Medal of Honor*.)

At his home in Kilgore, Jim Logan holds both of his medals of honor. He was the first recipient of the Texas Legislative Medal of Honor, which requires that a Texan from a Texas unit (the 36th Division, in Logan's case) must already hold a Congressional Medal of Honor. (Courtesy of David Stroud.)

T-Patchers marched inland, often meeting fierce resistance, as well as harsh weather. From the invasion at Salerno in September 1943 until the German surrender in May 1945, most units of the 36th Division experienced a 200-percent turnover in personnel. (Courtesy of the Texas Military Forces Museum at Camp Mabry, Austin.)

Late in 1943 and early in 1944, the 36th Division battled entrenched Germans in the mountains of central Italy. Mont Maggiore was called "Million Dollar Mountain" because of the artillery expenditure. Braving icy trails and zero-degree temperatures, T-Patchers captured Mount Sammucro, and a bloody battle at San Pietro climaxed the capture of Mount Lungo. A classic film, *San Pietro*, by Academy Award–winning director John Huston, immortalized the efforts of the T-Patch combat soldiers. Photographs show men of the 141st Division in January 1944 in defensive positions (above) and in chow lines with mess kits (below). (Courtesy of the Texas Military Forces Museum at Camp Mabry, Austin.)

HQ. CO. 141ST CHOW LINE, JAN. 1944

The advance of the Seventh Army was blocked at Monte Cassino, and the 36th was ordered to execute a flanking movement with a hastily planned night crossing of the Rapido River. But Germans were entrenched above the open valley, which was mined. Boats and inflatable craft were assembled to ferry T-Patchers across the river, but most of these vessels were destroyed by German artillery. (Courtesy of the Texas Military Forces Museum at Camp Mabry, Austin.)

WOUNDED BEING EVACUATED DURING THE ATTEMPTED

The ill-conceived and disastrous attempt to cross the Rapido River on January 20 and 21, 1944, cost the 36th Division almost 1,700 casualties. Wounded T-Patchers were carried from the riverside to aid stations. In a later action, when his company was about to be overrun, T-Patch medic George Gordon ripped off his Red Cross armband, picked up a carbine, and stood off the Germans, earning a Medal of Honor. (Courtesy of the Texas Military Forces Museum at Camp Mabry, Austin.)

An unidentified machine gunner mans his wooded position. (Courtesy of the Texas Military Forces Museum at Camp Mabry, Austin.)

WINTER CRISIS – GENERAL PATCH, 7TH ARMY COMMANDER, STOPS TO TALK TO 141ST MEN ON WAY TO THE FRONT.

The 36th Division was the backbone of the Seventh Army. Lt. Gen. Alexander Patch took over command of the Seventh Army in 1944, leading the invasion of southern France and the drive into Germany. General Patch is pictured (at left) speaking to T-Patchers of the 141st Regiment during the winter of 1944–1945. (Courtesy of the Texas Military Forces Museum at Camp Mabry, Austin.)

THE FIRST WAVE POISED IMPATIENTLY, READY TO GO IN FOR THE KILL

T-Patchers of the 141st Regiment comprised the first wave of "the other D-Day," August 25, 1944. Following a devastating naval and aerial bombardment, the 141st Regiment would hit the beaches of southern France at 0800. To the north, on June 6, the Allies established a beachhead in Normandy. In July, Gen. George Patton led a breakout at St. Lo, and as Germans were driven backward, they suddenly had to contend with another invading army from the south. (Courtesy of the Texas Military Forces Museum at Camp Mabry, Austin.)

Members of the 1st Battalion of the 141st Regiment moved in to land on Camel Blue Beach at the far right flank of the invasion target. Camel Blue was only 80 yards wide, barely enough space to land a single battalion, but Camel Blue was strategically vital, and despite heavy shelling, the T-Patchers landed and quickly drove the Germans from slopes overlooking the beaches. (Courtesy of the Texas Military Forces Museum at Camp Mabry, Austin.)

OVER ROCK-ENCRUSTED GREEN BEACH, NEARLY ALL THE
36TH DIVISION LANDED ON D-DAY.

The 2nd and 3rd Battalions of the 141st Regiment scrambled across rocky Green Beach. The 142nd and 143rd Regiments soon stormed ashore behind the 141st Regiment, throwing the defenders out of prepared positions while keeping T-Patch casualties low. The 26th Regiment began a rapid sweep inland. (Courtesy of the Texas Military Forces Museum at Camp Mabry, Austin.)

A supply ship is moving toward Green Beach. Although only 250 yards wide, Green Beach was shallow, and by D-Day Plus One, trucks, tank destroyers, and tons of supplies were disgorged onto this rocky beach. (Courtesy of the Texas Military Forces Museum at Camp Mabry, Austin.)

A Texas Lone Star flag, sent by Gov. Coke Stevenson, flies proudly over the impressive customs house gateway at Schweigen, Germany. Just below the flag, a chalked sign credits the 142nd Regiment as the first regiment through the archway as the 36th Division assaulted Hitler's vaunted Siegfried Line. (Courtesy of the Texas Military Forces Museum at Camp Mabry, Austin.)

Four Red Cross "Donut Dollies" served the 36th Division in France in 1944, operating out of a captured German vehicle. From left to right are Dorothy Boschen, Virginia Spetz, Jane Cook, and Meredyth Gardiner. (Courtesy of the Texas Military Forces Museum at Camp Mabry, Austin.)

A facetious saying suggested, "The German soldier fights for the Fuhrer; the Japanese for his Emperor; the Englishman for King and Country; the Russian for his Motherland; and the American soldier fights for souvenirs." Four T-Patchers pose with a souvenir Nazi flag. (Courtesy of the Texas Military Forces Museum at Camp Mabry, Austin.)

With German resistance crumbling, the 36th Regiment moved rapidly, reaching Landsberg on April 29, 1945. Festung Landsberg, where Hitler had been imprisoned in 1923–1924 and where he wrote *Mein Kampf*, now held political prisoners. The Nazis had jammed 1,400 starving prisoners into a facility designed for 500. T-Patchers at Landsberg examine dead prisoners, among the 11 million Europeans who died under Nazi incarceration. (Courtesy of the Texas Military Forces Museum at Camp Mabry, Austin.)

COL. JOHN J. ALBRIGHT, CO OF 143rd, WITH BATTALION COMMANDERS, RECEIVES SURRENDER OF GERMAN XIII CORPS.

Col. John J. Albright (second from left), with his battalion commanders, accepted the surrender of Germany's XIII Corps just before the final German capitulation. Colonel Albright commanded the 143rd Infantry Regiment of the 36th Division. During the final days of the Third Reich, T-Patch units took into custody Reich marshal Hermann Goering, field marshal Gerd von Rundstedt, air marshal Ritter von Greim, SS general Sepp Dietrich, and more than a score of other generals. (Courtesy of the Texas Military Forces Museum at Camp Mabry, Austin.)

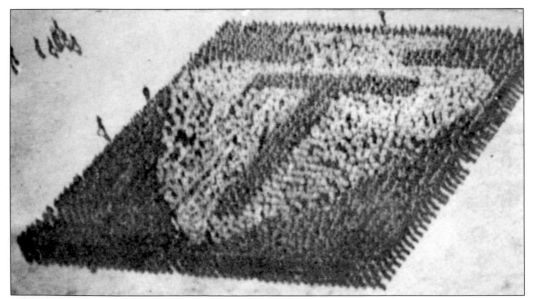

In the fall of 1945, four battalions of the 36th Division occupation troops formed an enormous T-Patch. By the end of the war, the 36th Division engaged in 19 months of combat, including two amphibious assaults in five campaigns. T-Patchers earned 15 Medals of Honor and captured 175,806 enemy soldiers. The 36th Division suffered 27,343 casualties: 3,974 killed, 19,052 wounded, and 4,317 missing in action. (Courtesy of the Texas Military Forces Museum at Camp Mabry, Austin.)

Troops of the 112th Cavalry advance ashore Arawe, New Britain

Several units that began as part of the 36th Texas Division were detached to the Pacific Theater. In 1944, the 112th Cavalry Regiment, operating as infantrymen, waded ashore at Arawa in New Britain. The Texans were quick to produce a Lone Star flag. Later the 112th Cavalry Regiment fought in the Philippines on Leyte and Luzon. (Courtesy of the Texas Military Forces Museum at Camp Mabry, Austin.)

Officers of Troop C gather around their Texas flag, Arawe, New Britain

After World War II, Audie Murphy was invited for a long stay at the Hollywood home of movie star James Cagney. Pursuing a film career, Murphy starred in westerns and in the 1956 hit *To Hell and Back*, the story of his war exploits. For several years, he simultaneously served the Texas National Guard. In 1953, during the Korean War, Captain Murphy (left) worked as a firearms instructor with members of the 36th T-Patchers. Murphy hoped to accompany them to Korea, but the division was not deployed. Although promoted to major, Murphy concentrated on his film career. At 46 in 1971, he was killed in a plane crash and buried with full military honors at Arlington National Cemetery. (Courtesy of the Texas Military Forces Museum at Camp Mabry, Austin.)

Six

TEXANS AT SEA

Adm. Chester W. Nimitz, commander in chief of U.S. Naval Forces in the Pacific (CINCPAC), was the architect of the strategy that swept the Japanese from their island strongholds and forced their surrender. Born in 1885 in Fredericksburg, Nimitz lost his father before his birth, but his grandfather, a German immigrant and former seaman, instilled strong character values. Intelligent and ambitious, young Nimitz applied for an appointment to West Point as a means of acquiring a college education. With no vacancy available, he instead obtained an appointment to the U.S. Naval Academy. As an officer, Nimitz became a leading submarine authority, building the submarine base at Pearl Harbor. He married and raised four children while advancing steadily through the steps to qualify for high command. (Courtesy of the National Archives.)

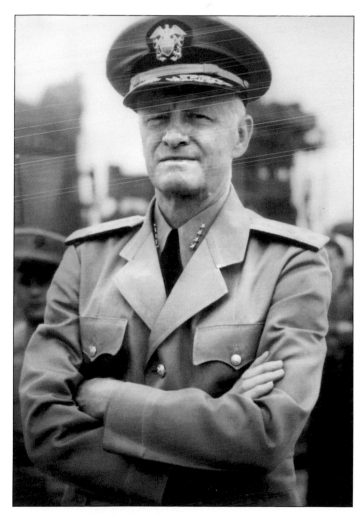

"Tell Nimitz to get the hell out to Pearl and stay there until the war is won." Pres. Franklin D. Roosevelt ordered Secretary of the Navy Frank Knox to send Admiral Nimitz from his post in the U.S. Navy Department to relieve Adm. H. E. Kimmel in the wake of the disaster at Pearl Harbor. During the next four years, Admiral Nimitz conducted the war in the Pacific with consummate skill. Under his command were hundreds of ships, thousands of planes, and hundreds of thousands of men, and with swelling strength, Admiral Nimitz relentlessly crushed the Japanese. On September 2, 1945, aboard the USS *Missouri* in Tokyo Bay, Gen. Douglas MacArthur (at left), acting as spokesman, signed the treaty with Japan as representative of the Allies. Admiral Nimitz, now wearing five stars, signed on behalf of the United States. (Both, courtesy of the National Archives.)

"Range 900 yards. Commenced firing. Expended four torpedoes and one Jap Destroyer." This classic expression of the U.S. Navy originated in a terse report from Comdr. Sam Dealey, the most decorated sailor of World War II. Born into a prominent Dallas family, he graduated from Oak Cliff High School and attended Southern Methodist University before entering the U.S. Naval Academy. Commanding the newly commissioned submarine *Harder*, Sam Dealey led six war patrols in 1943 and 1944. Using bold head-on tactics, Dealey was credited with sinking 16 Japanese vessels, including 4 destroyers, in five days. Dealey earned the U.S. Navy Cross with three gold stars, the Silver Star, a Purple Heart, and the army's Distinguished Service Cross. On August 24, 1944, the *Harder* was depth-charged with the loss of all hands. A year later, Dealey's widow was presented his Medal of Honor. (Courtesy of the National Archives.)

At Pearl Harbor, Dorie Miller (shown here wearing winter blues) performed heroically on the bridge of the sinking *West Virginia*. On May 27, 1942, Miller was awarded the U.S. Navy Cross at a ceremony for nine heroes aboard the aircraft carrier *Enterprise*. The first African American to win the U.S. Navy Cross, Miller was presented his medal by fellow Texan Adm. Chester Nimitz. (Courtesy of the National Archives.)

One of the first American heroes of the war, Dorie Miller was sent on a war bond speaking tour. He was stationed for several months aboard the cruiser *Indianapolis* before being transferred as a cook to the new escort carrier *Liscombe Bay*. In its first action, the ship exploded after being torpedoed by a Japanese submarine on November 24, 1943. Dorie Miller was 1 of 644 crew members who were killed. (Courtesy National Archives.)

Chuck Otterman (center) was a gunner's mate on the USS *Arizona*, his first ship after enlisting in the U.S. Navy in 1939. A star athlete in high school, he played on the battleship's football team. On Sunday morning, December 7, 1941, he said, "I was getting ready for church services on the fantail of the *Arizona*." Suddenly Japanese planes appeared, and an explosion blew the ship apart. Otterman and a shipmate swam to nearby Ford Island, where they obtained a motor launch and returned to pick up survivors. More than half of the 2,400 Americans who died at Pearl Harbor died on the *Arizona*. Otterman was placed on a burial detail, then assigned to the USS *Whitney*, a Pearl Harbor patrol boat. Later he was sent to Texas to join the crew of the USS *Murray*, a destroyer under construction at Orange, where he met his future wife. After 20 years in the military, Otterman returned to East Texas, serving as police chief at Center—and as one of the last survivors of the *Arizona*. (Courtesy of Donna Otterman Porter.)

Seabee Dick Bruton was 26 when the war started. Experienced in constructing highways, dams, and other heavy projects, he enlisted in the U.S. Navy and soon found himself on dangerous duty in the Pacific. With the Seabees, Chief Bruton helped build roads and airstrips while fighting raged nearby in Guam, Iwo Jima, and other combat zones. After the war, Bruton returned to Maud in Northeast Texas and raised a son and daughter. (Courtesy of Shirley Bruton Ford.)

Walter C. Todd, from rural Rusk County, was a graduate of Stephen F. Austin State Teachers College. Obtaining a commission in the U.S. Naval Reserve, Todd rose to the rank of lieutenant during the war. Lieutenant Todd served as gunnery officer aboard the El Caney, 1 of 481 T2-SE-A1 Liberty ships. The T2-SE-A1 was the workhorse of the tanker fleet, carrying nearly 65 million tons of oil to war zones on 6,500 voyages during the war. (Courtesy of Cliff Todd.)

Lt. (jg) Dan Sharpley was valedictorian of Corsicana High School and a graduate of Baylor University. As a young officer, he was assigned to Naval Intelligence. On duty in Brazil, Lieutenant Sharpley surrendered to a call to preach. After the war, he used his GI Bill to attend Southwestern Baptist Seminary, where he met Doris Allred, who committed to full-time Christian service after her husband, an airman, was killed during a training accident. Dan and Doris married and raised five children in Brazil, where they spent 30 years as missionaries. (Author's collection.)

Billie Gray Beason (left) was the wife of Curtis E. Beason, son of Mr. and Mrs. G. L. Beason of DeBerry in Panola County. Curtis was a private in the U.S. Army, his brother James was in the U.S. Navy, and their sister trained as a U.S. Army nurse. When Curtis was killed in France in 1944, his young widow promptly enlisted in the WAVES. (Courtesy *The Men and Women in World War II from Panola County*.)

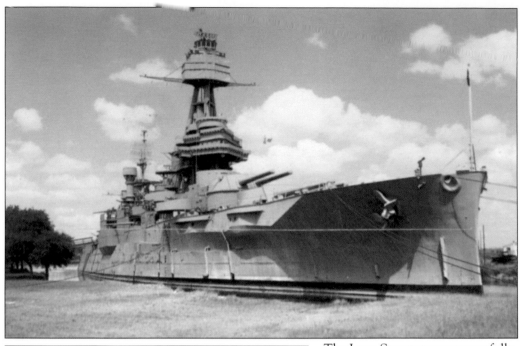

The Lone Star state was powerfully represented at sea during World War II by the battleship *Texas*. The USS *Texas*, BB-35, was a product of the dreadnought age. Its keel was laid in 1911, and the "Mighty T" was commissioned in 1914. The *Texas* is 573 feet in length with a 106-foot beam. Following service in World War I, the *Texas* was modernized during the 1930s. (Author's collection.)

The main battery of the *Texas* consisted of ten 14-inch guns in five turrets, with 70 men assigned to each turret. When U.S. forces invaded North Africa in 1942, the battleship bombarded shore installations. Similar fire support was provided in 1944 at the D-Day Normandy invasion and during later campaigning in southern France. Transferred to Admiral Nimitz's Pacific Fleet in 1945, the *Texas* bombarded Iwo Jima and Okinawa before ferrying troops home at war's end. (Photograph by the author.)

When the *Texas* was built, battleships were in no danger from the skies, but during World War II, radar units and antiaircraft guns were installed on every available surface space, causing a need for additional crew members. Below deck, therefore, stacks of bunks were added anywhere space could be found. In 1914, the *Texas* carried a crew of 944 enlisted men and 58 officers. By 1945, the complement had expanded to 98 officers and 1,625 men. (Photographs by the author.)

With a complement of more than 1,700 officers and men, the *Texas* was a floating city. A soda fountain ladled out ice cream and Coca-Cola to off-duty crew members. The ship's store, below, sold candy bars, chewing gum, cigarettes, and pipes to men of the *Texas*. (Photographs by the author.)

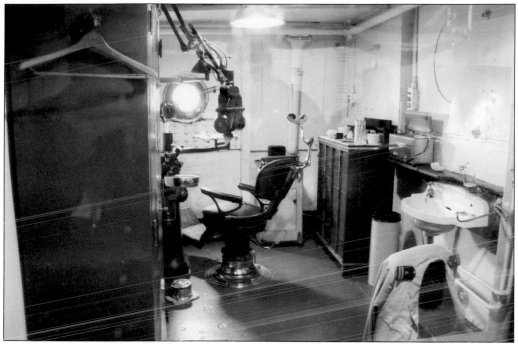

In addition to a large and well-equipped sick bay, the *Texas* also maintained a dental office. (Photograph by the author.)

In "officer's country," the officers shared a large wardroom and took their meals at tables with white tablecloths and napkins. (Photograph by the author.)

The interior of the bridge featured the ship's wheel and controls to signal the engine room. (Photograph by the author.)

The ship's office was operated by the first lieutenant and his staff. (Photograph by the author.)

The USS *Stewart* was the first destroyer escort built, launched, and commissioned at Brown Shipbuilding yards in Houston. Commissioned on May 31, 1943, the *Stewart* entered the Atlantic Fleet, escorting convoys to Europe and engaging in hunter-killer action against German U-boats. At right is a view of the bow gun and bridge. Decommissioned and mothballed in 1947, the *Stewart* eventually returned to the vicinity of its origins, becoming part of Seawolf Park in Galveston in 1974. (Photographs by the author.)

The U.S. Navy named battleships after states and cruisers after cities. The USS *Houston* was one of six heavy cruisers of the *Northampton* class commissioned in 1929 and 1930. With a top speed of 32 knots, the *Houston* mounted nine 8-inch guns in three turrets. On February 28, 1942, the day after participating in the Battle of the Java Sea, the *Houston* was battered by several Japanese warships. The *Houston* fought back furiously but went down with the loss of 693 men. (Courtesy of the U.S. Navy.)

Seven

THE HOME FRONT

A German POW branch camp was located at the San Augustine fairgrounds. A contingent of soldiers, housed in pyramid tents, served as guards. The ladies of San Augustine provided amenities for these soldiers, including a Thanksgiving dinner and dance on November 22, 1945 (prisoners were not returned to Germany for up to a year after the Nazi surrender). The event was held inside the fairgrounds exhibition building. (Courtesy of John and Betty Oglesbee.)

The government and the advertising industry allied to encourage women to enter the workforce during World War II. "Womanpower" was promoted through colorful, patriotic posters, as well as through radio spots and a variety of ads. Texas women responded with a sense of duty and adventure. In addition to 12,000 who donned uniforms, Texas women assumed roles in the workplace by the tens of thousands. (Author's collection.)

Women proved more efficient at certain war-related tasks, exhibiting greater patience and rapidity than men. Women of Terrell are folding parachutes, a task that had to be performed flawlessly. (Courtesy of the No. 1 BFTS Museum.)

The census of 1940 revealed that only 9 percent of American mothers held jobs outside the home. But the enormous industrial production of World War II, coupled with the severe manpower shortage, brought women into the workforce in great numbers. Most women returned to their homes after the war, but a trend had been started, and by 1976, more than half of American mothers had joined the workforce. (Author's collection.)

Citizens were urged at every hand to buy war bonds. The government needed vast infusions of cash to provide supplies for the war effort, such as planes, ships, tanks, jeeps, uniforms, guns, and munitions. Money was raised quickly through an unprecedented (and "temporary") withholding tax and through war bonds. Posters were everywhere, and moviegoers read war bond ads with the credits to each motion picture. (Author's collection.)

During World War II, for the first time in U.S. history, the American people were subject to rationing. Ration books were issued to all civilians, young and old. Even if a customer had the cash to purchase meat, sugar, gasoline, or tires, the required number of stamps had to be produced for the sale to be completed. There was considerable trading of different types of stamps, and a widespread black market developed. (Photograph by the author.)

The wartime speed limit was a sedate 35 miles per hour, which conserved gasoline as well as tire rubber. Tires and gasoline both were rationed, with most Texans limited to 3 gallons of gasoline per week. Gov. Coke Stevenson protested that gasoline was as necessary to Texans as "the saddle, the rifle, the ax, and the Bible." (Courtesy of the Nimitz Museum.)

There had been oil fields in Texas since the 1890s, and the largest was discovered in 1930 near Kilgore (pictured at left). The East Texas Oil Field was 42 miles long north to south and several miles wide—over 200 square miles—and every inch oozed black gold. By 1940, there were 25,000 wells across the field. (Courtesy of Gregg County Museum.)

More than 200 Texas counties produced oil. The Lone Star state produced 40 percent of U.S. oil and 25 percent of the world's oil, with a refining capacity that duplicated these percentages. Texas crude oil and refined products were shipped by tankers from the Gulf Coast to the Northeast, but German U-boats began sinking these tankers in the Gulf of Mexico, and within a few months, construction began on a great pipeline. (Courtesy of Gregg County Museum.)

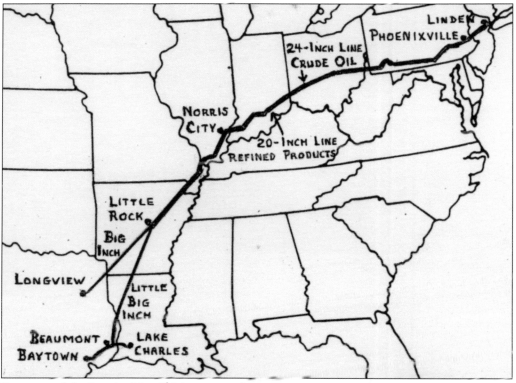

Secretary of the Interior Harold Ickes persuaded oil industry executives to plan what would become the largest pipeline in the world. Steel was in great demand, but Ickes finally obtained permission from the Federal Allocation Board. War Emergency Pipelines, Inc., a private company, handled construction, while the Reconstruction Finance Corporation provided funding that totaled $146 million. The "Big Inch," 24 inches in diameter, would transport crude oil, while the "Little Big Inch," 20 inches in diameter, would carry refined products. Construction began on the Big Inch in August 1942 and was completed the following February. The Big Inch was 1,254 miles long, from Longview to Phoenixville, Pennsylvania. The Little Big Inch, beginning in the refinery complex between Houston and Port Arthur, was built from January 1943 to March 1944. Over 300,000 barrels of oil per day were delivered to the Northeast—a total of 350 million barrels before war's end. (Courtesy of Gregg Country Museum; diagram by the author.)

The Todd Shipbuilding Corporation maintained shipyards in Galveston (pictured above) and Houston. Another Houston shipyard was operated by the Brown Shipbuilding Corporation. A total of 35,000 employees worked at these yards. Orange had three shipyards building destroyer escorts, wood-hulled minesweepers, and amphibious landing craft. Beaumont's Pennsylvania Shipyards built Liberty ships. (Author's collection.)

Sprawling airplane factories in Garland, Grand Prairie, and Fort Worth manufactured everything from AT-6 trainers to P-51 fighters to B-24 bombers. At least 500,000 rural Texans migrated to urban centers to work in airplane plants and shipyards, ammunition plants, and the petrochemical industry. Texas workplaces were also manned by more than 450,000 employees from out of state. (Author's collection.)

During the Republic of Texas, there was a large but loosely organized militia. During the Civil War, every man in the sparsely settled frontier counties was required to join the Texas Home Guard to battle Comanche and Kiowa raiders. Texas later fielded strong units in the National Guard, most notably the 36th Division. During World War II, members of the Texas State Guard wore a distinctive shoulder patch. (Courtesy of Keystone Square Museum, Lampasas.)

Texas State Guard Shoulder Patch
May 1943 - Present

As part of the World War II Civilian Defense program, the Texas State Guard was organized. Members of San Augustine's State Guard donned garrison caps and conducted drills with personal shotguns and rifles. (Courtesy of John and Betty Oglesbee.)

THE UNITED STATES OF AMERICA

VETERANS' ADMINISTRATION

WASHINGTON, D. C.

National Service Life Insurance

DATE INSURANCE EFFECTIVE ___ MAY 10, 1945 ___

CERTIFICATE No. N 18 877 012

This Certifies That ___ WILLIAM C. O'NEAL ___ FN ___

has applied for insurance in the amount of $ ___ 10,000. ___ , payable in case of death.

Subject to the payment of the premiums required, this insurance is granted under the authority of The National Service Life Insurance Act of 1940, and subject in all respects to the provisions of such Act, of any amendments thereto, and of all regulations thereunder, now in force or hereafter adopted, all of which, together with the application for this insurance, and the terms and conditions published under authority of the Act, shall constitute the contract.

Frank T. Hines
Administrator of Veterans' Affairs.

Countersigned at Washington, D. C.

June 12, 1945
(Date)

Registrar.

Mrs. Jessie L. O'Neal
Box 367,
Lampasas, Texas.

Insurance Form 360

The National Life Insurance Act of 1940, passed by Congress when the United States launched a substantial military buildup, provided a $10,000 life insurance policy for all servicemen. Immediately upon entering military service, soldiers and sailors designated a beneficiary, most commonly their wife or mother. If a man was killed in training or combat, his National Life Insurance policy paid $10,000 to his beneficiary. (Photograph by Karon O'Neal.)

Minor league baseball had been a vital part of the Texas sports scene since the late 19th century. The Texas League was founded in 1888, while the East Texas League (right, Tyler game program) and other minor leagues provided entertainment across the Lone Star state. Although the East Texas League halted operations in 1941, the Texas League was 1 of 30 minor leagues to play in 1942, the first wartime baseball season. But able-bodied men—including baseball players—were entering the service in large numbers, while travel restrictions added to the difficulties. The major leagues continued to play throughout the war, but only 10 minor leagues opened the 1943 season. Longtime Texas League president J. Alvin Gardner kept the league offices open in Dallas, but there was no play in Texas in 1943, 1944, and 1945. Stadiums such as Houston's Buffs Field (below) were closed until the end of the war. (Both, author's collection.)

Recruits were not supposed to enjoy family weekends during basic training. But Pvt. W. C. O'Neal, a graduate of Texas A&M (class of 1938) who grew up on a farm in Navarro County, was assigned to Fort Hood, 25 miles from his wife's hometown of Lampasas. His mother-in-law, who operated a photography studio, rented a room to the wife of a major stationed at Fort Hood. Weekly, the major arranged a rare weekend pass for Private O'Neal so that they could be ferried to and from Lampasas in the O'Neal family car. On one of these weekends in 1945, O'Neal posed for a photograph with his wife and two children. (Courtesy of Judy O'Neal Smith.)

Eight

POW CAMPS IN EAST TEXAS

During World War II, more than 425,000 Axis prisoners of war were incarcerated at over 650 POW camps across the United States. More than 50,000 of these POWs were housed in Texas at 22 base camps and 60 branch camps. About 48,000 Germans were held in Texas, along with 2,500 Italians and 1,000 Japanese prisoners. Base camps in East Texas included Tyler's Camp Fannin, Fort Crockett in Galveston, Camp Hearne, Camp Maxey near Paris, and Camp Mexia. East Texas branch camps included Alto, Alvin, Anahuac, Angleton, Atlanta, Bay City, Bryan, Center, Chireno, Corsicana, Harmon General Hospital in Longview, Kaufman, Kirbyville, Liberty, Lufkin, Navasota, Orange, Patroon, Princeton, and San Augustine. The POWs pictured at Camp Hearne are attending an English language class. (Courtesy of the Hearne Chamber of Commerce.)

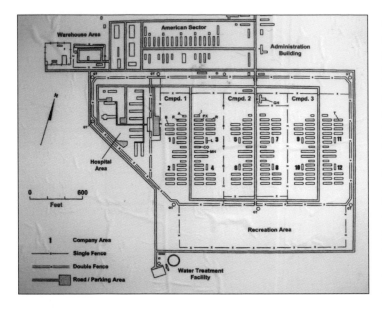

Camp Hearne was built on a 720-acre site just north of town. Construction of this POW base camp began in September 1942 and was completed within six months. There were three POW compounds, a hospital area, a recreation area, and an "American sector" for the force of 500 guards. Over 4,800 Germans were incarcerated at Camp Hearne, which also acquired a few hundred Japanese POWs in mid-1945. (Courtesy of the Hearne Chamber of Commerce.)

There were regular assemblies in the compounds for roll call and announcements. But this formation was for a funeral. A flag-draped coffin is being carried by eight men to the camp cemetery northeast of the compound. About a dozen POWs died of illness or accidents, two committed suicide, one was murdered, and one was shot while trying to escape. (Courtesy of the Hearne Chamber of Commerce.)

114

Camp Hearne had the unique distinction of being the headquarters of the German Postal Unit in 1944 and 1945. The Camp Hearne Postal Unit received and distributed letters and parcels from Germany for German POWs anywhere in the United States. The volume often soared above 40,000 letters and parcels daily, and 22 buildings in Compound 1 were utilized by the postal unit, which organized three eight-hour shifts six days per week. (Courtesy of the Hearne Chamber of Commerce.)

According to the Geneva Convention, POWs who were officers or noncoms could not be required to do manual labor (which is why all American combat airmen held the rank of sergeant). Therefore, most of the work in Camp Hearne compounds was done by about 20 percent of enlisted men, while ranking POWs were kept busy with recreational pursuits, including building model gliders. This pose is behind the band shell of Compound 2. (Courtesy of the Hearne Chamber of Commerce.)

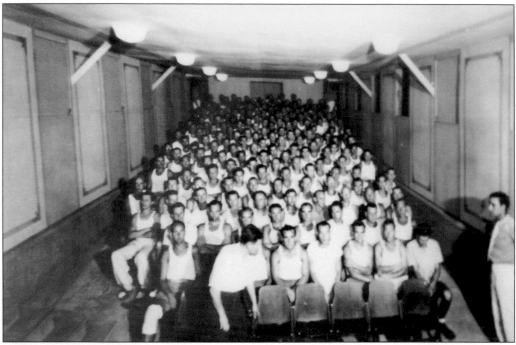

POWs converted a 100-foot-by-20-foot recreation building into a theater, complete with a stage and orchestra pit. Germans assembled for a performance, with the front row usually reserved for American officers and guards. (Courtesy of the Hearne Chamber of Commerce.)

A former POW at Camp Hearne recalled that "we had all kinds of talented guys, including actors, musicians, and so on." Therefore, there was a great variety of shows in the theater, including a western performance. Note the actor at left in a Lone Ranger mask, and at right, the sign "Jesse James Gang." (Courtesy of the Hearne Chamber of Commerce.)

The Camp Hearne water tower, although rusty, is still on-site among the foundations and other remnants of the old POW facility, which closed in January 1946. (Photograph by the author.)

Among the old streets and foundations of the American sector of Camp Hearne are three fire hydrants, still reddish in color and bearing the date 1942. (Photograph by the author.)

Lufkin is the only Texas community to house two POW camps. There was a desperate need for manpower in the East Texas timber industry. Southland Paper Mills leased an abandoned Civilian Conservation Corps camp in November 1943. Necessary renovations were completed by February 1944, a few weeks after a severe ice storm rendered the immediate salvage of lumber and pulpwood a necessity. Camp No. 1 housed 300 Germans, who were paid 80¢ per day to produce pulpwood. The POWs liked working outdoors for pay, and in April 1944, Camp No. 2 opened for 500 more POW laborers at the fairgrounds south of town. The CCC gate at Camp No. 1 is pictured above, while below, a POW poses beside stacked timber. (Above, photograph by the author; below, courtesy of John and Betty Oglesbee.)

German POWs at the San Augustine Camp worked industriously in the surrounding pine forests for the rate, set by the government, of 80¢ per day. The POWs preferred to leave confinement for work in forested regions that were similar to their homeland. A group of POW laborers poses beside a work truck. (Courtesy of the Hearne Chamber of Commerce.)

The San Augustine POW Camp was a branch camp under the base of Camp Fannin in Tyler. The San Augustine Camp was located at the fairgrounds. The exhibition building was converted into a mess hall, but the prisoners and guards lived in pyramid tents. (Courtesy of the Hearne Chamber of Commerce.)

During the 1930s, the only U.S. prison for women was in West Virginia. It was decided to construct a federal women's reformatory on an 833-acre plot provided by the City of Seagoville. Opened in October 1940, the redbrick facility, featuring Colonial-style buildings, sidewalks, and spacious lawns, resembled a college campus more than a prison. The capacity of 400 was quickly reached, but in 1942, these women were moved to West Virginia so that the penal institution could become an internment camp for Japanese—from Peru. Latin American countries deported Japanese immigrants, and the United States accepted them as possible bargaining pawns for the exchange of American citizens captured by Japan. The six dormitories at Seagoville were comfortably furnished, a female doctor administered a well-staffed hospital, recreational activities were varied, and with more than 640 internees, 50 one-room cabins were installed. (Courtesy Seagoville Public Library.)

Nine

WHERE TO GO AND WHAT TO SEE

After the war, the USS *Texas* was mothballed near Baltimore, and by 1948, there were plans to use the old battleship as a bombing target. But the citizens of Texas raised funds to save the "Mighty T," and in 1948, the U.S. Navy towed it to Texas. Transferred to the state in ceremonies at the San Jacinto Battleground on San Jacinto Day in 1948, the *Texas* became the nation's first memorial battleship. The *Texas* is moored within sight of the 570-foot-tall San Jacinto Monument. (Photograph by the author.)

In Greenville, the Audie Murphy/American Cotton Museum celebrates America's most decorated soldier of World War II, as well as the area's rich cotton heritage. Audie was born and raised on cotton farms in the area. He worked in Greenville as a teenager, and in June 1942, just after his 18th birthday, he enlisted at the U.S. Army Recruiting Office in the basement of the post office. A 10-foot bronze statue of Murphy dominates the memorial in front of the museum. (Courtesy of the Audie Murphy/American Cotton Museum.)

The entrance to Fredericksburg's sprawling National Museum of the Pacific War is the Steamboat Hotel, complete with crow's nest and flagpole, and built in 1852 by the grandfather of Chester Nimitz. Chester was born in a house across the street and was raised in the landmark hotel. The museum tells the story of Admiral Nimitz and the entire war in the Pacific. It is a must for World War II buffs. (Photograph by the author.)

A statue of Gen. Dwight David Eisenhower, supreme commander of Allied Expeditionary Forces in Europe, dominates the approach to the house where he was born in Denison. Ike's father was a railroad employee and rented the house, shown in the background, where his third son was born on October 14, 1890. The presidential birthplace includes a museum. (Photograph by the author.)

In Austin, Camp Mabry, a center of the Texas National Guard, houses the Texas Military Forces Museum. After entering the gate, the military buff has the pleasure of driving through most of the 375-acre compound before reaching the museum. Displays include a strong focus on the 36th Division during World War II, and outside Armor Row and Artillery Row are dozens of tanks, destroyers, other vehicles, and artillery pieces. (Photograph by the author.)

The Lone Star Flight Museum is packed with World War II aviation treasures. Pictured in the foreground is a Vought Corsair, workhorse carrier fighter of the Pacific. The Lone Star Flight Museum, which also contains the Texas Aviation Hall of Fame, is located at Scholes International Airport in Galveston. (Photograph by the author.)

The B-25 medium bomber achieved immediate fame after the Doolittle Raid on Tokyo. A B-25 is part of the impressive collection of World War II planes at Cavanaugh Flight Museum at Addison Airport. In Northeast Texas there are other flight museums with World War II exhibits and planes, including the Frontiers of Flight Museum at Dallas's Love Field and the Historic Aviation Museum at Tyler's Pounds Field. (Photograph by Dusty Henderson.)

The USS *Lexington* Museum on the bay in Corpus Christi is a superb World War II naval museum. The fleet carrier *Lexington* was sunk during the Battle of the Coral Sea, on May 8, 1942. The next year, a newly commissioned carrier took the name of the heroic old ship. The new *Lexington* was in action from Tarawa to Tokyo, and the "Lady Lex" was the first carrier to enter Tokyo Bay after the Japanese surrender. (Photograph by Katie Rash.)

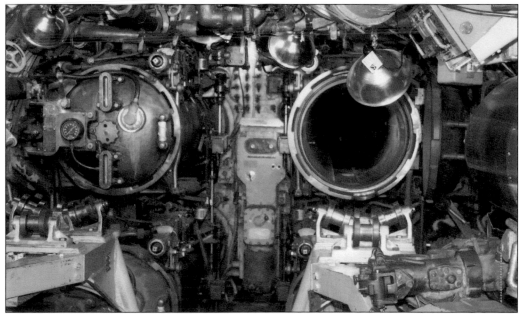

At Seawolf Park on Galveston's Pelican Island, visitors may tour the USS *Stewart*, the first destroyer escort built in the nearby Brown Shipyards and one of only five destroyer escorts left in the world. (The *Stewart* is described and pictured in Chapter 6.) The submarine USS *Cavalla* is also open for tours, permitting visitors to experience the cramped confines of a World War II sub. Pictured above are the forward torpedo tubes. (Photograph by the author.)

The sentry station at the gate of No. 1 British Flying Training School at Terrell now welcomes visitors to the No. 1 BFTS Museum. The museum impressively relates the little-known story of RAF flight training in East Texas, and constant expansion is ongoing. (Photograph by the author.)

This replica of a POW barracks houses the Camp Hearne Museum. Scheduled to open in September 2010, the barracks stands among the old streets, foundations, and fire hydrants of the big POW base camp. (Photograph by the author.)

There are World War II monuments on courthouse squares all across East Texas, such as this handsome statue in front of the ornate Hopkins County Courthouse in Sulphur Springs. Almost all county and community museums, even in small towns, have good exhibits of World War II artifacts and photographs. Outstanding collections are on display at the Texas Heritage Museum at Hill College in Hillsboro, at the Military Museum of Texas in Houston, and at the Bob Bullock Museum in Austin. (Photograph by the author.)

The World War II Memorial was erected in 2007 on the state capitol grounds, a short distance northwest of the capitol building. The monument honors the 23,022 Texans who died in military service during the war, as well as the 830,000 Texans who served in uniform. Across the sidewalk is a monument erected by Texas Pearl Harbor survivors, and elsewhere on the grounds is a granite T-Patch monument to the 36th Division. (Photograph by the author.)

DISCOVER THOUSANDS OF LOCAL HISTORY BOOKS FEATURING MILLIONS OF VINTAGE IMAGES

Arcadia Publishing, the leading local history publisher in the United States, is committed to making history accessible and meaningful through publishing books that celebrate and preserve the heritage of America's people and places.

Find more books like this at
www.arcadiapublishing.com

Search for your hometown history, your old stomping grounds, and even your favorite sports team.

MADE IN THE USA